No Tears *in Heaven*

THE 1926 BARNES-HECKER MINE DISASTER

by Thomas G. Friggens

A *Michigan History* magazine Heritage Publication

Michigan Historical Center
Michigan Department of History, Arts and Libraries
Lansing, Michigan
2002

Other heritage publications from
Michigan History magazine:

Michigan Soldiers in the Civil War
Father Marquette's Journal
Michigan and the Civil War: An Anthology
African Americans You Need to Know
Makin' Music: Michigan's Rock & Roll Legacy

Visit *Michigan History* magazine and its growing family of
heritage publications on the World Wide Web:
www.michiganhistorymagazine.com

No Tears In Heaven
by Thomas G. Friggens
Third Edition
ISBN 0-935719-54-7
© 2002 Michigan Historical Center; Michigan Department of History, Arts and Libraries
First published 1988

Printed on recycled paper.
This product was not printed at Michigan taxpayer expense.
MHM-33 (rev. 9/02)

Michigan Department of History, Arts and Libraries
William M. Anderson, director

Michigan History magazine is part of the Michigan Historical Center, which is part of the
Department of History, Arts and Libraries. Dedicated to enhancing the quality of life in Michigan,
the department also includes the Mackinac Island State Park Commission, the Library of Michigan,
the Michigan Film Office, and the Michigan Council of Arts and Cultural Affairs.

"God shall wipe
away all the tears
from their eyes.
There shall be no
tears in heaven."

—Reverend Hugo Hillila, Finnish Lutheran Church
Ishpeming, November 1926

t 7:20 A.M., in the chill gray dawn of Wednesday, November 3, 1926, the day shift reports to work at the Barnes-Hecker iron mine in Michigan's north-central Upper Peninsula. The men arrive from neighboring communities—Diorite, Ishpeming, North Lake, South Greenwood, Barnes-Hecker Location. They are immigrants and sons of immigrants; fathers, sons, brothers and friends. Their faces reflect the weariness of their labors and the pride of their heritage. They are strong and alive, laughing and sullen, as they prepare to toil underground. For them it is a routine beginning to a day like all others. Overhead the skies are unsettled; there is a prediction of snow. It has been an unusually wet autumn and there is talk among miners of an early winter.

Elsewhere is news of yesterday's election. Fred W. Green, Republican mayor of Ionia, has outpolled Detroit Democrat William A. Comstock in the state's gubernatorial race. At midnight the governor-elect announces, "I shall mix common sense and old-fashioned honesty with twentieth-century business methods and, God willing, hope to achieve some substantial contribution to good government in Michigan." But strong government, in Michigan and throughout the country, seems now to be in recess. The decade roars with whimsy. The Charleston is the dance rage; the fashion for women is short hairdos and hemlines; and the national preoccupations are prosperity, Prohibition and amusements.

In the eight years since the end of the World War, the United States has emerged from a sharp recession and sustained a growing prosperity. The nation's industrial production climbs as income grows and the cost of goods declines. The Republican presidential administration supports a high tariff, tax reduction and industry. In the succinct words of President Calvin Coolidge, "The chief business of the American people is business."

In 1917, the Cleveland-Cliffs Iron Company salvaged the defunct Chase Mine's head-frame for use at the Barnes-Hecker Mine.

The chief business of Michigan's central Upper Peninsula is the production of iron ore. The discovery of Michigan's iron wealth in the mid-nineteenth century coincided with unprecedented national growth. The quality and quantity of Michigan iron was unrivaled through the 1890s, when the state produced 43 percent of the nation's ore. But by the turn of the century, as the extraction of high-grade iron ore from Michigan's underground mines became more difficult and costly, vast new reserves developed in Minnesota outpaced their eastern neighbors. Nonetheless, Michigan's annual production surpassed 18 million tons in 1916. Despite a slump in 1921, ore production now exhibits steady growth.

From the opening of the Marquette range in 1845 to the early 1870s, the Michigan iron industry was pioneered by small companies with limited capital. However, depressions in the late nineteenth century forced scores of independent mines to merge with powerful companies. In 1926 three Cleveland, Ohio, corporations—Cleveland-Cliffs, Pickands-Mather and M. A. Hanna—dominate the industry.

A property of the Cleveland-Cliffs Iron Company (CCI), the Barnes-Hecker tract was first explored using diamond drilling in 1907. Cylindrical cores cut by this rotary drill provided samples of subsurface strata, located ore bodies and revealed the nature of the overburden through which a shaft was sunk. Although the Barnes-Hecker deposit was modest and its overburden swampy, development proceeded in 1917.

Construction of the mine was not without problems. The shaft was sunk through a "very heavy quicksand." Though the mine is lined with concrete to prevent caving earth, miners sometimes experience "sand runs" through underground fissures. Construction crews also encountered a large volume of water. Unable to determine the source or to keep pace by pumping, mine engineers controlled the problem with a series of underground dams. Suspecting that surface water also contributed to the problem, the company emptied nearby North Lake and drained surface water from the vicinity of the Barnes-Hecker ore body via a trench three and a half miles long and several feet deep. These extraordinary efforts reduced the volume of water pumped from the mine by nearly 80 percent, from 3,000 gallons per minute to 700. The former swamp overlying the ore deposit is now dry.

Since it began production in 1922, the Barnes-Hecker Mine has produced nearly 400,000 tons of ore. Its production of 182,038 tons this year accounts for 4 percent of the total ore shipments from the Marquette range. The rusted steel headframe, salvaged from the defunct Chase Mine in 1917, dominates the mine's surface facilities. Other structures include the mine office, electric plant, engine house, stockhouse and workshops. In the dry—a modern changehouse equipped with steel lockers, showers and latrine—miners at the start of their shift take off their street clothes and put on work garb stained red with ore. The track and trestles of the Lake Superior and Ishpeming Railroad, a CCI subsidiary, link the mine with Marquette's ore docks some 23 miles to the east.

Beneath the headframe the vertical mine shaft descends 1,060 feet. Access is by electric cage (elevator) or an enclosed ladderway. Horizontal drifts (tunnels mined from the shaft toward the ore body) are worked at depths of 600, 800 and 1,000 feet. They are connected by a network of sublevels and raises (inclined passageways). At the end of the third level, some 2,000 feet distant from the shaft, a raise descends 200 feet at 45 degrees to connect with the sixth level of the Morris-Lloyd Mine, a mile and a half to the southeast.

The soft hematite ore mined here is extracted by a common practice called sublevel caving. Sublevels extending from each main drift

This mat of logging at the Negaunee Mine illustrates part of the caving method of mining used at Barnes-Hecker.

William Tippett (left), considered one of CCI's best mine captains, works today with his two brothers and their stepbrother. Pumpman Peter Mongiat (right) is working a double shift to cover for an absent coworker.

are mined out, then filled with timber lagging and cross-lagging. Timbers supporting the roof are blasted down, causing each sublevel to collapse, forming a compact mat of interlaced timber and rock engineered to withstand a sudden rush of earth or water in a cave-in. Mining is now under way two sublevels above the first level.

Those who toil in the manmade caverns beneath the surface of the Barnes-Hecker property are representative of the industry's labor force. Michigan's iron industry employs some 12,000 workers. It is an immigrant workforce, chiefly composed of men from Canada, the British Isles and Scandinavia.

Ethnic diversity is reflected in the languages, urban demography and social traditions of the iron ranges. "Almost all the tongues on the face of the earth are represented in this class of workingmen," an observer noted. "The visitor to this mining country finds it the most cosmopolitan society he has ever entered."

Walter Tippett's first day of work at Barnes-Hecker is November 3, 1926. He is shown here in April 1926.

The Barnes-Hecker workforce numbers 150 men, employed in two shifts. Among the 50 or more who go underground today, three out of five are immigrants. The remainder, with two exceptions, are Michigan natives. There are 35 miners on this shift. With them are trammers, motormen, stemmers and pumpmen. Their average age is 36 years. Four in every five are married, and most have children. Two miners, Thomas J. Kirby Sr. and Edwin Chapman, share this shift with their sons. The elder Kirby, a veteran miner and bass drummer, is among Ishpeming's best-known musicians. George and Richard Lampshire are brothers. Walter Tippett, age 31, is the former night captain of the Marquette police force. He recently resigned his position as a guard at Marquette State Prison to accept employment here. Today, Tippett is alert with anxiety as he begins his first day on the job. His underground supervisor is his 43-year-old brother, William Francis Tippett, who is among the company's best mine captains. Tippett's other brother, Albert, and young step-brother, Rutherford John Wills, also work this shift.

Today, newlywed John Heino returns to work after a brief honeymoon. Peter Mongiat Sr., a 43-year-old pumpman, is working a double shift in place of an absent coworker. Despite his wife's urgings to stay home to stock firewood, Emil Maki, father of seven, decides to haul fuel next Sunday. He misses his bus, so he drives the family automobile to work.

Maki's drive from his residence at Cliffs-Shaft Number 75 in Ishpeming is less than five miles. Sixty percent of the Barnes-Hecker day shift resides in this town. Marquette County boasts a population of nearly 45,000 people. Ishpeming, its largest city, supports ten schools, two banks, a 1,200-seat opera house, a business college, a public hall and a Carnegie public library with 29,000 books. The city, lighted by gas and electricity, also boasts eight iron mines, two hospitals, three hotels and four theaters and vaudeville houses.

Led by President William Gwinn Mather, CCI pioneered mine safety programs in 1911.

Nearer the mine are the villages of North Lake and Barnes-Hecker Location, communities built and operated by the mine company to provide inexpensive housing for its employees. Barnes-Hecker Location, a quarter-mile east of the shaft, is among the region's most attractive mining locations. Rows of duplexes line a wide boulevard that circles a park of trees. All have running water and electricity. Stands of conifers and hardwoods have been preserved to lend beauty.

There are no stores; a schoolhouse enrolls 33 students. The young family of Nels Hill rents residence Number 13 at a cost of $9.50 per month. In house Number 21, mine captain William Tippett and his wife make monthly payments of $19.50 for rent, $3.50 for electricity and 50 cents for water.

Across Michigan's Upper Peninsula, iron-mining companies have long provided their employees with a variety of social services through company towns, including inexpensive housing, medical care and the convenient marketplace of the company store. Although this system of benevolent paternalism may create excessive company control over the lives of employees, there is little evidence that major firms in the Upper Peninsula exploit the situation. Corporate leaders, such as Cleveland-Cliffs president William Gwinn Mather, are motivated by sound economic logic. "Employers of labor," one business leader says, "are beginning to understand the economic value of human life, and the importance from a business standpoint of protecting and caring for their employees."

Mather's CCI is a pioneer of this philosophy. The company sponsors classes in the English language, citizenship and naturalization for employees who are recent immigrants. It promotes home improvements, supports practical education in the schools and provides recreation halls and bathhouses replete with bowling alleys, theaters and meeting rooms. Since 1894, CCI has awarded annual prizes for the best-kept grounds, homes and gardens. More important, it has operated a welfare department since 1905, providing financial assistance during extended illness, for medical treatment and after death. Pension and visiting nurse programs were added in 1909, safety programs two years later.

Despite these safety programs, mining remains a dangerous vocation. Accidents result in deaths and scores of injuries each year. Premature and missed blasts, the collapse of overhead rock and falls into shafts are the principal causes of mine fatalities. Materials dropped down shafts, the collapse of staging and defective hoist cables are other causes. Some accidents are attributed to the failure of immigrant workers to comprehend warnings and instructions in English,

In the early years of the twentieth century, this North Lake neighborhood (shown above in the mid-1980s) is home to many CCI miners and their families.

others to inexperienced workers. Many accidents result from carelessness.

Gradually, however, both government and business have taken action to improve safety in the mines. In 1886, Michigan created the office of county mine inspector. Since 1911 safety practices by mine operators have significantly reduced accidents. A company official noted, "No longer is the economic phase of mining regarded as paramount. Equal in importance has become the slogan 'Safety First.'" Cleveland-Cliffs has pioneered mine safety through its safety department and Safety First campaigns. William Conibear, safety inspector since 1911, also serves as secretary of the firm's safety inspection committee. This group, which includes top management personnel, superintendents and department heads, disseminates safety regulations and recognizes mines with exemplary safety records. Conibear brings more than three decades of mining experience to this task and advocates accident prevention through investigation, education and invention. He visits the mines monthly, inspecting equipment, hoists, cages, skips, ladderways, ventilation, fire hazards, first-aid facilities and general working conditions. Mine workers are not forewarned of his visits. "I go unheralded," he states.

Accompanied by mine captain Tippett and Marquette County mine inspector William E. Hill, Conibear last inspected the Barnes-Hecker Mine three weeks ago. He knows most of the miners by name.

CCl's safety inspector since 1911, William Conibear conducts monthly inspections at the Barnes-Hecker Mine.

It is his practice to observe their work and to question them about their working conditions.

Barnes-Hecker is considered a safe mine by all. There has been just one fatality, a carpenter, since the property opened in 1917. Experienced shift bosses such as Sam Phillippi inspect work areas twice per shift, exhorting their crews to observe caution.

Bruna Phillippi and Rutherford Wills (seated) are wed in 1926. Sweethearts Margaret Tippett and Joseph Mankee (standing) are the couple's maid of honor and best man.

Notwithstanding such precautions, accidents occur. Last month Phillippi's son-in-law, Rutherford Wills, was pinned between the motor (haulage locomotive) and a pocket of rock. The motorman escaped serious injury but had to be hospitalized. This morning, he is on the day shift.

Wills hired on at the Barnes-Hecker Mine in 1923. He has worked one year on the surface, two years underground. On this day he reports to the second level, 800 feet below the surface. As a motorman, Wills operates one of the mine's three underground electric haulage locomotives, which pull loaded ore cars to the shaft where the ore is emptied by chutes into a skip and raised to the surface.

At age 22, Wills is tall, lean and in excellent physical condition. A native of Quinnesec, he is newly wed to Bruna Phillippi and resides near her parents' home at Barnes-Hecker Location. He operates the motor with brakeman Jack J. Hanna. Hanna, 23 years old, returned to his native Ishpeming from Detroit in July and has been employed at the Barnes-Hecker Mine only three weeks. More than a dozen others—miners, trammers and timbermen—work on the second level.

Newlywed Thomas J. Kirby Jr. operates the bell signals and the skip loading chutes on Barnes-Hecker's first level.

Two hundred feet above them miners labor on the first level, which is 1,700 feet from the shaft. Walter Tippett and three others work by the light of carbide lamps on a sublevel some distance below the main drift. Thomas J. Kirby Jr., who operates the bell signals and skip loading chutes near the shaft, is working with five other miners on the first level. Kirby is 24 years old. A former railway worker, he

Brakeman Jack J. Hanna, age 23, has worked at Barnes-Hecker for only three weeks.

quit his job last year to work at the mine. Seven weeks ago he married Bertha Seablon, a corset factory employee in Ishpeming.

Others descend 1,000 feet into the dim, craggy passages of the third level. Here, the miners' world echoes with the staccato blows of pneumatic drills, the hiss of compressed air and the heavy blast of explosives. The smell of damp earth permeates these manmade tunnels, despite natural ventilation that flows through the shaft and the raises connecting the three main drifts.

Because his wife needs their car, North Lake Mining District superintendent Charles J. Stakel decides not to conduct his scheduled weekly inspection of the Barnes-Hecker Mine today. Instead, Captain Tippett accompanies county mine inspector Hill underground. A native of Finland, the 39-year-old Hill is respected by both mine officials and laborers. Yesterday, he was elected to a second term in office.

As Tippett and Hill inspect the working areas of the mine, the routine of Barnes-Hecker's day shift is unbroken. At 11:05 A.M. the officials pass Wills on their tour of the second level. One level below, Allivyon Miners completes repairs on an underground car and pauses to inspect ore chutes in the skip pit. Employed as track and car repairmen, Miners and his partner, Santoke Combelli, have been working all morning. Shortly after 11:00 A.M., they ascend the shaft and leave the mine.

On the third level, pipe foreman Edward Hillman has labored for three hours repairing pipe deep in the mine. Completing his work, he ascends to the first level where his next task will take him to the far end of the drift. Hillman pauses to ask the time. It is 11:20 A.M.

There is not enough time before dinner for him to begin a new job at the end of the drift, so he rides the cage up the shaft. As the cage approaches the surface, its occupants are buffeted by a rush of air. The sensation is brief. Hillman, a veteran miner, disregards it as a windstorm. Once he is on the surface, he walks away from the shaft.

On the second level, Wills and motor brakeman Hanna begin a final trip through the drift before breaking for dinner. From the workings above comes the muffled blast of explosives. Wills and his partner, overtaken by the air blast, stop the motor and dismount. Within seconds a stronger blast knocks them to the damp rock floor, extinguishing their lamps. Shaken by his fall, Wills scrambles to his feet and shouts to Hanna above a thunder of trembling earth, "I think we better get out of here!"

In a hurtling rush from somewhere above, a torrent of sand and water pours into the first level, foaming down the raises and shaft that connect the three main levels. There is little warning. Throughout the mine, electric lights dim, flicker and die as power is cut.

On the surface, Hillman and Allivyon Miners realize there is trouble underground. To Miners it is "something like a big wind in the shaft," possibly a broken air line. Hillman closes the main air valve. But the roaring underground continues. He tries unsuccessfully to ring the third-level pumphouse and then the first and second levels. The line is dead. Hillman and Albert Tippett descend the shaft to investigate.

On the second level, Wills and Hanna grope their way in the dark toward the shaft, guided by the feel of their rubber-toed boots against narrow-gauge track. Wills reaches the ladder leading to the third level. His impulse is to climb down and seek refuge in the concrete pumphouse below. He grapples with indecision, proceeds 30 yards toward the shaft, then returns to the ladder that leads deeper into the mine. As the air pressure blocks his ears to a rolling thunder of earth and water, instinct turns him back toward the shaft. With Hanna trailing, Wills shouts a warning to his close friend, Joseph Mankee. He urges the others to run and takes the lead. Reaching the shaft, where mud and rock now plummet from above, the men start up the vertical ladder. They are 800 feet from the surface.

Elsewhere in the mine, Captain Tippett, Inspector Hill and a small party of miners are cut off from the shaft. They make their way in darkness through the third level. Their only avenue of escape is the raise that connects with the Morris-Lloyd Mine. Some 300 feet above them,

19

Wills and his companions race against death. The ladder rungs and his gloves are greased with mud. Wills slips, regains his grip, jerks his gloves from his hands with his teeth and resumes climbing. Reaching the first level, he momentarily breaks pace and calls to Thomas Kirby Jr. to get out. Kirby swings onto the ladder behind him as Hanna and Mankee reach the first level. Below them a seething mass of water, mud and debris swiftly fills the shaft.

Wills opens a lead on his companions. Through the din he hears their shouts. Suddenly a massive object hurtles down the shaft, narrowly missing Wills and shattering the ladder below him. In seconds Kirby, Hanna and Mankee are overtaken by the rising maelstrom. Wills climbs frantically as the whirlpool clutches his boots. The water rises as fast as he can climb.

Three hundred feet below the surface, Hillman and Albert Tippett, descending the shaft to investigate, meet Wills scrambling up the ladder. They pause, firing questions: What has happened? Is anyone else coming up? Wills gasps that Mankee, Hanna and Kirby are behind him. Hillman shines his light down the ladderway and calls into the darkness. There is no response. He senses "a heavy pressure of air coming" up the shaft. As the three men begin their ascent, a terrifying crash rends the shaft some distance below.

At the surface, Miners notes the crash, "just like a big wind." With concern for Hillman and Albert Tippett foremost in his mind, he descends by ladder some 250 feet, where he meets the others. He lights their way to the surface. It is 11:30 A.M. when Wills pulls himself from the mine shaft and collapses to the frozen earth, exhausted and cramped with muscle spasms.

Mine superintendent Stakel is underground at the Morris-Lloyd Mine when word of the accident reaches him. Once on the surface, Stakel telephones the Barnes-Hecker office for details. He quickly changes from his mine clothes, commandeers a car and speeds to the scene, where shrill steam whistles signal the emergency.

Details of the accident emerge from the initial confusion. There are reports of a cave-in the size of a city block and 60 feet deep. It is southeast of the mine shaft, directly above the workings. The mine is rapidly filling with fine "quicksand," water and debris. Between 40 and 65 men are believed trapped.

S. R. Elliott, assistant general manager of mines, is in Crystal Falls, some 50 miles distant. Notified by telephone that a serious accident has occurred, he leaves immediately for the scene. At Republic, 15 miles to the southwest, CCI safety inspector Conibear is told of the accident at 12:30 P.M. Conibear arrives at Barnes-Hecker within an hour. By then the water level has risen to within 185 feet of the surface. There is no hope for survivors. The flood now threatens the neighboring mine. Safety First and medical teams from other mines and communities are summoned.

It is 2:00 P.M. when Elliott arrives. With a small group of experts he assesses the situa-

S. R. Elliott, CCI's assistant general manager of mines, drives from Crystal Falls to assess the damage at Barnes-Hecker.

tion. Convinced that there are no survivors, he orders that bailers and pumps be brought in to empty the mine of water.

By 3:30 P.M. mud and water in the shaft begin to recede as the cave-in area on the surface backfills with water. Deep in the mine, debris has plugged the outlet to the Morris-Lloyd shaft. Unofficial reports from the mine office confirm that Wills is the lone survivor. In Marquette an extra edition of *The Daily Mining Journal* mistakenly reports 65 deaths.

At 4:00 P.M. Conibear and four supervisors probe the mine from the sixth level of the Morris-Lloyd shaft. They proceed by motor until debris blocks their path. Now Conibear and another man push on.

William Huot (left) and Thomas J. Kirby Sr. (right) are among the seven men whose bodies were recovered from Barnes-Hecker's third level.

They cautiously step from logs to lagging strewn in mud and sand waist deep. Perhaps 1,000 feet from the raise connecting the two mines they discover the first body, half-buried in mud. Conibear recognizes his hunting companion and friend, William Tippett. Nearby are the bodies of Inspector Hill and Thomas Kirby Sr. Four others are found nearer the raise. They are battered almost beyond recognition, stripped of clothing and entangled in debris. It is evident that the seven bodies were dragged some distance before the violent torrent spent its force. At about 8:00 P.M. the bodies are brought to the surface, laid upon a machine-shop floor and gently washed with water from a garden hose.

Beneath the steel headframe of the Barnes-Hecker Mine, the families and friends of the entombed miners keep a hopeful vigil awaiting release of the victims' names and word of their fate. Beneath the glare of lights, onlookers raise their collars against the chill night air, pull hats lower and thrust hands deeper into pockets. Escaping blasts of air from the flooded mine shaft burst upon the night.

Word that William Tippett's body is among those recovered is carried to his mother by her son-in-law, John Wallberg. In quiet disbelief she murmurs from her seat, "John, have you ever suffered like I am suffering now?"

She is not alone in her grief. The impact of Michigan's worst mine accident strikes the whole community. In Ishpeming an observer remarks, "Never in the history of our city has there been such wide-spread sympathy." Another notes, "There are more sorrow-stricken homes . . . now than ever before at one time." Yet another muses, "All that remains is to mourn the victims, comfort . . . their families and see, as time clears the picture, what, if any, lesson is to be learned from it."

One hundred thirty-two minor children are left father-less; four out of five are 15 years old or younger. Four victims leave widows with seven children; two others leave six children; and in several other bereaved families there are four and five children. At Barnes-

Hours after the cave-in, onlookers and anxious relatives wait for word on the fate of the missing miners.

Hecker Location, Bruna Phillippi Wills mourns her father, while Margaret Tippett, the maid of honor at Wills's wedding just two months ago, suffers the double loss of a parent and sweetheart.

Arvi Wepsela, at age 18 the youngest victim of the accident, was the sole supporter of his parents and six siblings. Widower Richard Lampshire, at age 35, leaves four orphans; his brother, a victim at age 28, was single. Their sister, Mrs. Earl J. Ellersick, also grieves her husband. She now must support her four children and the orphans of her brother.

There are 42 widows. Among them are Florence Verran Hanna, who married Wills's brakeman less than a year ago in Detroit, and Bertha Seablon Kirby, the bride of Thomas Kirby Jr. In her honeymoon cottage near Ishpeming, Tynne Alto Heino, married just two days, exchanges her wedding gown for a mourning dress. She weeps openly as wedding furniture arrives at her door.

Near the door of the William Huot residence in North Lake, a badge of black crepe is placed beside shaded windows. At age 38, Huot is survived by his wife and seven children. When his aged mother, herself

Michigan's worst mine disaster leaves 132 young children fatherless and widows 42 women including members of the Santti, Koskinen, Lehtimaki, Laituri and Kallio families.

near death with diabetes, is told of her son's demise, she responds, "I know he has gone to prepare a place with God for me." She then lapses into a coma.

The Cleveland-Cliffs Iron Company quickly appoints a trained medical team to assist the victims' families. The day after the disaster, a physician and four company nurses visit each bereaved home, extending sympathy and assurances of aid in the days and weeks ahead. In addition to immediate relief, CCI plans—beyond its legal responsibility—the economic rehabilitation of those families deprived of wage earners. The company will pay beneficiaries the maximum pension under Michigan's Workmen's Compensation Law, $4,200 in 300 weekly allotments. Although legally ineligible as dependents of a public officeholder, the family of Inspector Hill is added to CCI's compensation payroll. Relief also comes from

Myrtle Welander is among the team of CCI visiting nurses sent to care for the dead miners' families.

25

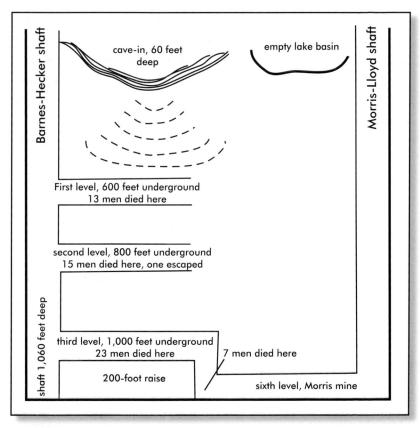

The cave-in occurs 1,000 feet from the Barnes-Hecker shaft; the Morris-Lloyd Mine is approximately two miles distant. This diagram is not drawn to scale.

the American Red Cross, the City of Ishpeming and the Ishpeming Women's Service Club.

Social workers find courage mixed with grief in the homes of dead miners. Sent to bring solace, they are themselves inspired repeatedly by widows who rally their children. In one home a mother bends over her sewing. Visiting nurses ask how they can help. She responds, "I have been trying to get the clothes sewed for the children, but I don't seem to be able to hurry." Stubbornly blinking back tears, she turns to her visitors. "Do you think I could borrow some clothes for the children? I want them to look nice when they go to their father's funeral."

On Thursday, news of the Barnes-Hecker disaster is spread across the nation's front pages. The Associated Press and newspapers from Detroit, Chicago, Milwaukee and Duluth have dispatched correspondents to the scene. A small press corps sends thousands of words over the wires. At its Ishpeming office, Western Union assigns extra operators to the task. Poignant images are captured through the lens of Tom Bennett, an Ishpeming photographer commissioned by *The Daily Mining Journal.* Kenneth R. Eddy is dispatched to the scene by the Pathé Picture Corporation to film a newsreel report. In Ishpeming, the editor of the *Iron Ore* warns against yellow journalism. "The facts are sad enough," he writes, "without any untruthful, sensational additions."

At the mine, reclamation work has proceeded throughout the night. A safety zone holds onlookers at bay. Several thousand people have already visited the scene. The state police control the curious. All who visit the mine venture to the cave-in site a

The Barnes-Hecker cave-in site, shown here in 1927, is approximately 60 feet deep.

quarter mile distant. What was yesterday a gaping dirt pit is now a cold lake, fringed with scarred earth and uprooted trees.

Determined to recover the entombed bodies of its employees, CCI has asked volunteer crews, led by its most experienced men, to repair the Barnes-Hecker shaft, which has been stripped by the rush of sand and water to within 375 feet of the surface. Water in the mine shaft continues to recede, permitting cautious investigation at greater depths. Five hundred feet below the surface a mass of broken timbers, likened to a "gargantuan game of jack-straws" 40 feet thick, blocks progress.

Water in the shaft has fallen to within feet of the first level. Before the drift can be breached, however, timber, water and hard-packed sand must be laboriously removed and the mine shaft repaired. The danger of further flooding remains high, and

This scene from the funeral of one of the victims is repeated many times in Ishpeming. The city's streets and churches overflow with mourners and sympathetic onlookers.

a surface crew prepares to drain the cave-in area by pump in an effort to lower water in the shaft.

Two days after the disaster, CCI convenes a meeting of 24 industry representatives and engineers, including representatives from the U.S. Bureau of Mines, to review the accident. After careful analysis, they conclude that "the mine was operated according to the best mining practice . . . and the accident was due to causes that could not have been foreseen."

The magnitude of the cave-in baffles observers. Some blame a wet overburden, saturated by the excessive rainfall of the past season; others, a collapsed swamp. Mine engineers attribute it to a ruptured vug, a large underground reservoir that extended close to the surface and was ripped open by explosives. Assistant general manager Elliot will later testify:

> *We never had anything to fear at all; we never dreamed that anything like this could happen, and in fact no satisfactory explanation has been given for it. How that could break through the surface and such a tremendous amount of stuff come in there without the slightest warning is more than I or anyone else can explain. . . . It is something absolutely beyond us.*

There is no public hint of culpability, nor criticism of a company that has pioneered mine safety for 15 years.

On November 5 a hushed crowd gathers outside the William Hill residence as his widow and four young children trail the casket to the waiting hearse. At a front window, Hill's aged mother parts a lace curtain to watch. As the funeral cortege departs for Ishpeming's Finnish Lutheran Church, where 700 people await the public service, the curtain cannot shield her grief.

Similar scenes are repeated this weekend at the funerals of six others recovered from the mine. Among them are William Tippett, William Huot and Thomas Kirby Sr. Neighbors and strangers alike donate automobiles for the motorcades that carry the bereaved and jam Ishpeming streets. Thousands of mourners overflow the churches, and many stand outside in reverent silence. From the pulpit of the Finnish Lutheran Church, the Reverend Hugo Hillila officiates at the triple funeral of Arvi Wepsela, Nels Hill and Henry Haapala. He consoles mourners in both Finnish and English and promises, "God shall wipe away all the tears from their eyes. There shall be no tears in heaven."

Still mourning the loss of her husband in the Barnes-Hecker cave-in, Mrs. Delia Trudell sits with seven of her eight children shortly after the disaster.

On November 22, 1926, Kenneth Eddy's *Pathé Weekly* newsreel premiers at the Ishpeming Theater. The film features scenes of the mine shaft and cave-in area; victims' homes and families; the lone survivor, Rutherford Wills; and the funeral of Inspector Hill.

Efforts to reclaim the mine continue for more than two months. The shaft is repaired to the depth of 600 feet, and the first level is entered. Twenty minutes after the crew is ordered out, on November 20, 1926, a dam breaks and the mine again fills with water. Engineers unanimously agree that the mine is unsafe. On January 11, 1927, CCI announces that the mine will be abandoned.

Cleveland-Cliffs seals the mine with concrete, dismantles the buildings and relocates the houses of Barnes-Hecker Location. It compensates each dependent family twice the amount originally announced— $8,400 in 300 weekly allotments of $28 each. The company also provides free rent and utilities to widows and offers employment to the victims' sons upon their eighteenth birthdays. Rutherford and Bruna Wills move to Flint in the spring of 1927. Wills experiences recurring nightmares of his ordeal until his death in 1973.

On January 13, 1927, the Michigan legislature rejects a resolution calling for an investigation of the accident. The following month a coroner's inquest rules "that the deceased met their death in the Barnes-Hecker mine by a cave-in, the cause of which is unknown."

On Memorial Day, funeral services for the miners who remain entombed are held at the site of the worst mine accident in Michigan history.

Those who died in the Barnes-Hecker Mine disaster.

Full Name	Marital Status	Age	Birthplace	Family Residence	Surviving Children Under 16 Years Old
Herman Aho (miner)	M	36	Finland	Dexter	0
Peter Carlyon (miner)	M	64	England	Ishpeming	0
Raymond Carlyon (motorman)	S	22	Michigan	Ishpeming	-
William Henry Carlyon (miner)	M	54	New Jersey	Ishpeming	0
Edwin Herman Chapman (miner)	S	22	England	Ishpeming	-
Edwin John Chapman (miner)	M	46	England	Ishpeming	5
Thomas Drew (trammer)	S	41	England	Ishpeming	-
Peter Durocha (pumpman)	M	38	Michigan	South Greenwood	5
Earl John Ellersick (trammer)	M	28	Pennsylvania	Ishpeming	4
Gust Albinus Franti (miner)	M	38	Finland	Ishpeming	1
Joseph Gelmi (miner)	M	38	Italy	South Greenwood	5
James Anthony Greene (trammer)	M	33	Michigan	Ishpeming	0
Henry Haapala* (miner)	M	38	Finland	Diorite	3
John Joseph Hanna* (miner)	M	22	Ishpeming	Ishpeming	0
John Arvid Heino (miner)	M	25	Finland	Ishpeming	0
Nels Hill (miner)	M	27	Finland	Barnes-Hecker Location	2
William E. Hill* (county mine inspector)	M	39	Finland	Ishpeming	4
Willian Huot* (miner)	M	39	Michigan	North Lake	7
Frank Jokinen (miner)	S	44	Finland	Ishpeming	-
William Kakkuri (trammer)	S	23	Michigan	North Lake	-
John Arvid Kallio (miner)	M	35	Finland	Ishpeming	2
Thomas James Kirby Jr. (miner)	M	23	Ishpeming	Ishpeming	0
Thomas James Kirby Sr. (miner)	M	59	England	Ishpeming	1
Theodore Kiuru, (miner)	S	24	Michigan	Ishpeming	-
Uno Koskinen (miner)	M	22	Michigan	Ishpeming	0
John Edwin Laituri (miner)	M	43	Finland	Ishpeming	2
George Washington Lampshire (miner)	M	28	Michigan	Ishpeming	1
Richard Henry Lampshire (miner)	M(wid.)	35	Michigan	Ishpeming	4
John Isaac Luoma* (stemmer)	M	23	Michigan	Ishpeming	1
Emil Matthew Maki (miner)	M	38	Finland	Barnum Location	5
Joseph Mankee* (miner)	S	22	England	Barnes-Hecker Location	-
Walter Mattila (miner)	M	29	Finland	Finland	2
Peter Mongiat (pumpman)	M	43	Italy	Barnes-Hecker Location	5
Solomon Myllimaki (trammer)	M	48	Finland	Ishpeming	3
Sam Phillippi (shift boss)	M	54	Italy	Barnes-Hecker Location	1

Full Name	Marital Status	Age	Birthplace	Family Residence	Surviving Children Under 16 Years Old
William Harry Quayle (miner)	M	52	England	Ishpeming	0
Elias Ranta (miner)	M	42	Finland	North Lake	6
John Santti (miner)	M	37	Finland	Barnes-Hecker Location	4
James Scopel (trammer)	M	36	Italy	North Lake	3
Clement Simoneau (trammer)	M	29	Michigan	Negaunee	0
Nestor Sulonen (miner)	M	42	Finland	Finland	2
Eric Timo (or Timoharju) (miner)	M	49	Finland	Finland	7
Walter Tippett (stemmer)	M	31	Michigan	Ishpeming	4
William Francis Tippett* (mine captain)	M	43	Republic	Barnes-Hecker Location	0
William Henry Toumela (trammer)	M	30	Michigan	Ishpeming	1
Louis Joseph Trudell (miner)	M	44	Michigan	Ishpeming	7
Nicola Valenti (miner)	M	32	Italy	South Greenwood	7
Solomon Valimaa (miner)	M	44	Finland	North Lake	6
John Arvi Wepsela* (miner)	S	18	Diorite	Diorite	-
Albert Wickman (miner)	S	33	Finland	Ishpeming	-
John Wiljanen (miner)	M	47	Finland	Ishpeming	2

Spelling varies among three primary sources: Marquette County records of deaths, *The Daily Mining Journal* and the Cleveland-Cliffs Iron Company *Annual Report* (1926). The county death record is most reliable.

* bodies recovered

This monument, located at the Michigan Iron Industry Museum near Negaunee, remembers the men who died in the Barnes-Hecker Mine disaster.

ABOUT THE AUTHOR Thomas G. Friggens is regional supervisor for the Michigan Historical Museum's four Upper Peninsula field sites, which include the Michigan Iron Industry Museum. He holds degrees in history from Albion College (B.A., 1971) and Wayne State University (M.A., 1973). He and his wife, Mary, live in Marquette and have two sons, Christopher and Michael.

MICHIGAN IRON INDUSTRY MUSEUM The Michigan Iron Industry Museum explores more than 150 years of life and work on Michigan's iron ranges. The museum overlooks the Carp River in Negaunee, site of the first iron forge in the Lake Superior region. The museum, open May through October, offers visitors of all ages exhibits, outdoor interpretive paths and special events and programs. The Michigan Historical Center now plans a museum expansion that includes additional exhibit space, classroom and multipurpose facilities, outdoor interpretive areas and the  restoration of the 1860s mine haulage locomotive *Yankee*. Admission is free. For information, telephone (906) 475-7857.

BIBLIOGRAPHIC NOTE Primary sources include testimony taken at the February 2, 1927, coroner's inquest, Marquette County, Michigan; 1926 death and marriage records, Marquette County, Michigan; records of the Cleveland-Cliffs Iron Company, Barnes-Hecker Donations, 1927-32; *The Annual Report of the Inspector of Mines for Marquette County* (1927); Department of Conservation, *Mineral Resources of Michigan* (1922 and 1928); and the *Ishpeming Iron Ore, The Daily Mining Journal, The Detroit News* and *The New York Times*. Secondary sources include Gardner A. Wallberg, "The Barnes-Hecker Mine Disaster," undated manuscript; Charles J. Stakel, "Barnes-Hecker Reminiscences" in *Jaspilite* (1972); *Red Dust*, edited by Bobbi Ameen, Maxine Honkala and Sharon Richards (1985); and Thomas G. Friggens, "Michigan Iron: A Historical Survey of the Michigan Iron Industry," (1986), manuscript, Michigan Department of State, Bureau of History.

PHOTO CREDITS Superior View/Marquette (front cover, pages 9, 24, 27); Marquette County Historical Society (pages 6, 14, 16, 17, 21, 22, 23, 25, 26, 28, 30); Dewey B. Tippett (pages 10, 15); Michigan Iron Industry Museum (page 8); Cleveland-Cliffs Iron Company (page 12); Thomas G. Friggens (page 13); Tom Buchkoe/Marquette (Page 33).

ACKNOWLEDGEMENTS *No Tears In Heaven* was produced by the staff of *Michigan History* magazine, Dr. Roger L. Rosentreter, editor; Carolyn Damstra, assistant editor; Kristin M. Phillips, marketing manager; Kelley Plummer, circulation; and Mary Jo Remensnyder, administrative assistant. Design and electronic production: Holly Miller, Salt River Graphics/Shepherd.

BARNES-HECKER
Memories of a Misfortune

Fifty-one men left home for work at the Barnes-Hecker Mine one cold, November day in 1926, never to return. They were fathers, brothers and sons. Now hear their stories as told by their descendants in this Michigan Association of Broadcasters award-winning documentary produced by WNMU-TV, Northern Michigan University.

Only
$19.00
Plus $4.00 shipping

Order from the Michigan Iron Industry Museum, 73 Forge Road, Negaunee, MI 49866. Telephone **(906) 475-7857**